Church Music
and the Other Kinds
A Musical Manifesto of Sorts

Church Music
and the Other Kinds

A Musical Manifesto of Sorts

Douglas Wilson

canonpress
Moscow, Idaho

Douglas Wilson, *Church Music and the Other Kinds*
Copyright ©2014 by Douglas Wilson

Published by Canon Press
P. O. Box 8729, Moscow, Idaho 83843
800-488-2034 | www.canonpress.com

Cover design by James Engerbretson.
Interior design by Valerie Anne Bost.

Unless otherwise indicated, all Scripture quotations are from the King James
Version.

Table of Contents

Introduction

Music is far more central to our lives than we perhaps assume. We come into contact with music all the time—sometimes explicitly as in worship, and sometimes implicitly as with the background music in restaurants that you scarcely notice, and other times explicitly (but still thoughtlessly), as with the music that many have loaded on their iPhone.

How can we relate the music of our worship services to the music we enjoy throughout our lives? Should there be such a relation?

Two points then, to begin with. The first is that worship is a particular kind of event, and God has fashioned the world in such a way that different kinds of music accompany different kinds of events. You don't expect a Sousa march at a third-graders birthday party, you don't expect a little ragtime piano piece for the offertory in church, and you don't expect a soft string lullaby as the troops are assembling for battle. Occasions differ radically, and God has created music with the flexibility to suit virtually every kind of occasion. So when we emphasize a particular kind of music in our worship of God, it should not be assumed from this that we disparage or have contempt for other kinds of music. There is a time and place for virtually everything.

But there is an error that can flow from this, if we are not careful. We don't want "church music" everywhere else, and we don't want thrasher metal here. But there is a great danger, especially in these schizophrenic times, for us to assume that church music is the Lord's music, and that when we go off to do our own thing, that all bets are off, that you can listen to whatever *you* want. But the Lordship of Christ extends throughout all your days, and not just on the Lord's Day. And though church music is not to be every kind of music, whatever you listen to throughout the week should be *consistent* with what we sing here in church. Why is this? Can fresh water and brackish water flow from the same spring?

We are Trinitarians, and so the musical world is before us, with numerous lawful genres waiting for us— blues, rock, jazz, classical, country, bluegrass, operatic, and so forth. It is a big world. But music that spits out hatred for God and contempt for women, to take just one all too common example, is not a lawful genre . . . and it is not consistent with the worship of God on Sunday morning.

CHAPTER 1

Appropriate in Worship

We began by noting that worship is a particular kind of occasion, and so it requires a particular kind of music. Related to this was the point that not all our music has to be church music, but that all of it should be fundamentally consistent with what we sing here in church.

We come now to the next point, which is that the questions of what kind of music is appropriate for worship, and what constitutes a legitimate determination of consistency between that worship and what you listen to or play throughout the course of the week, is a challenging and demanding question. And this means that "personal taste" plays a much smaller role in this than many of us would like to believe. In short, the phrase "but I like it" is not, as many believe, the end of all discussion, but perhaps rather the beginning of the discussion.

Of course we should like the music we sing, but we should like it for reasons, and, if I may push it this far, we should like it for *good* reasons.

But in a culture dominated by individualism, personal taste can never be questioned. It is the final refuge in which everyone may, if they so wish, hole up. It is the final refuge in which they may disappear under the headphones.

But those good reasons include the teaching and requirements of Scripture, the creational mandate found in the ways that the triune God gave His law to the sound waves as they strike the ear, the fitness of the music to the occasion apart from the lyrics, and of course the suitability of the lyrics to the music. This represents just a small handful of the many considerations that have to be brought to bear. This is another way of saying that this is an area in which musical expertise is to be *valued*.

At the same time, we should all remember Mark Twain's joke about the music of Wagner being better than it sounded. In the last several centuries, more than one expert has composed some gosh-awful things. One of the things that the Reformation recovered was the active and intelligent participation of the congregation in worship: When congregations are trained and informed, as they ought to be, this is in part so that the congregation has a *right* to their opinion.

CHAPTER 2
What Music Cannot Say

I n Psalm 22:3, we are told that God is holy, and that He *inhabits* the praises of Israel. What does that mean? We are the people of God, and when we sing, when we praise God, we are constructing a dwelling place for Him.

So what kind of place should we build? How should it be furnished and decorated? The Bible tells us that our praise of God should overflow as a function of the Word of God dwelling in us *richly*.

A common misconception in our day says that music is content-neutral, as though it were a universal sauce that can go with any meal. This idea arises from the fact that music is not as capable as language in communicating specific meanings. But just because it cannot communicate in as focused a way does not mean that it is not communicating at all. Music adorns words, and music must adorn words in ways that are consistent. Music is more general than the words, but they both still have to line up. The words cannot be specific—Des Moines—and the music the wrong kind of general—Wyoming, say.

Music cannot tell you the temperature at the airport, or that Washington crossed the Delaware, or that Jesus rose from the dead. But when words are expressed in poetry, and set to music, it must be music that communicates something general that is consistent with the specific meaning. Music can be exultant, romantic, goofy, melancholic, and so forth. So one of the central principles of church music is this—since we are building a habitation for the Lord in our praises, and He will condescend to live in what we sing, the way we adorn the house must be consistent with what we are saying the house is. If our words are to be reverent, holy, jubilant, loud, and grateful, then so must the music be.

CHAPTER 3
Standing Before Kings

We have noted earlier that Psalm 22:3 says that God lives in the praises of His people. He *dwells* there. This means that our songs, our psalms, our hymns are the living stones of a glorious Temple. This means that our music is a cloud of glory, the same kind of cloud that God used to display His glorified presence in the Temple.

This means that we must not be apathetic or listless in how we sing. If you were invited to sing for the queen of England, would you slouch as you did so? If you were asked to sing the national anthem before a ball game, would you do it with your chin on your chest? Would you mumble?

The complaint registered by the prophet Malachi is appropriate here (Mal. 1:8). When the people were bringing defective animals as a sacrifice to *God*, the prophet asked what the governor would think if you tried that stunt with him. The answer is *not much*, and it is curious that we would all think twice about offering some slipshod gift to a human dignitary—but we have to be reminded to offer our best to God of all creation. What does this say about us? If you were asked to make a gift for the president, one that would be on display in the Smithsonian, would you make a little box out of Popsicle sticks?

Proverbs says that if a man excels in his work, he will stand before kings. This is true of earthly kings, but it is also true of the king of all heaven. We have been summoned. This is a command performance. And He has said that in His grace, He is willing to inhabit, *dwell* in, the praises we offer up to Him. Now it is clear He is a God who stoops—He was willing to dwell in a manger at one point. But if we are preparing a place for Him, we must not arrange that kind of place for Him deliberately.

CHAPTER 4
Musical Instruments

I n Ephesians 5, the apostle Paul requires musical instrumentation in worship. He says there that we are
to be "speaking to [one another] in psalms and hymns
and spiritual songs, singing and making melody in
[our] heart to the Lord" (Eph. 5:19). The translation *in*
the heart would better be rendered as *with* the heart.
We would say "singing and making melody with all our
hearts." This is not an arbitrary choice; we can tell this
contextually. The short phrase "making melody" is a
rendition of a word that means to pluck a string—*psallo*.

Going over a song in our hearts is something we have
all done. Singing silently can be done—even though it is
frustrating, and is always looking for an outlet. But very
few of us have played the oboe in our hearts, or played a
trumpet or piano there. Doing that kind of thing is way
too close to playing air guitar. Telling the Ephesians to
play the violin in their hearts would be a little bit odd.

So Paul tells the Ephesians to sing and play stringed
instruments—just the kind of thing that the psalmist

would exhort Israel and all the nations to do. This is music out loud. But the driving force of the exhortation reveals the motive for instruments, and the motive for robust singing. We are told to sing *with all our hearts*. This kind of heart attitude looks around for ways to make it better, richer, louder. The same kind of thing comes out in Colossians. As the word dwells in us richly, the music should come out richly. A rich interior life cannot result in a poverty-stricken musical expression.

We want to worship God. We have music before us that is designed to help us with this. We should stand on the balls of our feet, eager to express in song what we believe God has done for us. After all, He is worthy.

CHAPTER 5
Music As Creational Gift

L et us continue to meditate on the role of music in our worship of God. But if we are to do this, we need to settle something early on. We worship God using means that He has given us in order to worship Him. When we worship God, we are returning something to Him. Nothing appropriate that we offer to Him originates with us. God has created us with the functional ability to worship Him. The innate capacity to do what He summons us to do is built into us. We must mature in these things, develop in them, grow in our sanctification, but we are honing a gift already given.

One example is language—hardwired into the very nature of the human brain. Another example is music—man is musical by nature. This also is hardwired in us. There has never been a race of men without music. This is a function of the created order. But just as some of us develop their talents for language, so also some develop their musical talents. This is well and good, but when the Bible summons us to sing, it assumes that *all* of us will be doing so. Everything that has breath is to praise the Lord. We do not want some who play and sing, and others who merely listen any more than we want some to speak and others to be mute. All of us are created to be musicians at some level.

If we deny or resist this, we are making room for evolutionary thinking about the nature of man, and the resultant musical relativism. But chord patterns and structures are not arbitrarily assigned by us; rather they are discovered and manipulated by us. And when we discover rightly, what we discover "answers to" the very nature of the world, the deepest desires of the human heart, and it resonates within the triune glory of God. God has made us to sing and play, and He has made us to sing and play *so that He might listen to us.*

It is therefore to be one of our highest priorities to value what we offer as much as He values receiving it. If God did not want to hear us from musically, He would not have commanded us to sing to Him with psalms and hymns and spiritual songs.

CHAPTER 6

Relativism Is Out

I n our congregation, we say the Apostles Creed each week. As we do, we confess that we believe in God the Father Almighty, Maker of heaven and earth. This refers to the doctrine of *creatio ex nihilo*, creation from nothing. Only God can create from nothing; it is one of the characteristics of Deity.

But Genesis does not say that God created a glob of inchoate stuff, but rather that He created heaven and earth, sea and dry land, sun, moon, and stars. When He created the world, He *designed* it to run and function a certain way. The world is not just here because God put it here, and that's all we have to learn from the doctrine of creation. No, every aspect of the world is engineered to certain ends. We learn what those "ends" are through careful study of the Scriptures, and careful study of the world itself in the light of Scripture.

The earth is the Lord's, and everything in the world is good in itself. But to appeal to this unquestionable truth as justification for putting beans in your ears, smoking dope, or playing random chaotic noises that some call music, is to be guilty of a very elementary fallacy. God made the world, certainly, but He also wrote the manual. How could the fact that Kitchen Aid manufactured your mixer be an argument for working up a small batch of concrete in it?

The rudiments of music are embedded in the way the world is. We learn from both Scripture *and nature* that a certain kind of music is for dancing, and another for mourning. Another kind of music calms the spirit, and another kind rouses the spirit. If you were asked to make an heirloom cabinet for the queen, you wouldn't use rough cut plywood. And if summoned to confess your sins musically before the Lord, you wouldn't use a bouncy little ragtime piece.

This means that at the very beginning of our study of music, we have to start by rejecting every form of relativism. Far too many Christians evaluate music on the basis of lyrics alone. Every wise craftsman who seeks to exercise true dominion in the world knows two things: first, he has creative authority to arrange—he is the craftsman. And two, he must respect the nature of the material he is using. The craftsman does not just exercise authority; he also *submits* to the nature of his material. This is true of all artisans, and of musicians particularly. And you, as part of the congregation of the Lord, are musicians before Him.

CHAPTER 7

Representative Musical Leaders

Worship is a solemn and joyful occasion, and so our music should match that kind of occasion. This means that we need musicians to teach and lead us. At the same time, in the ordinary course of things, we the people of the congregation, *not* musical experts, are to be the ones offering the sacrifice of praise.

This does not mean that those among us who are particularly gifted cannot offer music to God themselves—without the rest of us flatting and sharping along behind them. But when choral music by trained musicians is offered, we should be keeping two things in mind.

When this happens in the worship service, the musicians are functioning as our representatives. They are not ministers or angels of God, come down to sing *to* us. They are chosen from among us to sing to God. We should hear and listen with intelligence, so that we are able to say *amen* when they are done. This is why, when a piece is in a foreign tongue, we should provide a translation in the bulletin. This is why we want to increase musical literacy throughout the congregation, so that we can say *amen* to the music as well as to the words. Music itself, distinct from the words, is filled to overflowing with theological content, and we have a responsibility to understand something about it. The musicians are functioning on our behalf as they lead us. It is the same as when someone leads in prayer, and the rest of us say *amen*.

But there is a second thing. We also want our musicians to sing and perform in other settings, not just in this service of covenant renewal. In those settings—special performances, concerts, and so forth—we want to learn how to listen with wisdom so that we might grow and mature in our musical understanding. This will have an effect when we come to sing on the Lord's Day. For example, listening to a theology lecture in the course of the week is not formal worship, but, done right, it is an enormous help to you in worship. As a result, you come to worship God on the Lord's Day with more *texture* in your background. It is the same with music.

You should want everything you do in the course of the week to be helping you prepare for worship, because worship should be preparing you for everything you do in the course of the week. And keep in mind the point made earlier. It is *not* the case that all our music must be "church music." There are all kinds of secular music that can contribute appropriate texture to what you have to offer the Lord. But also keep in mind that we live in a confused and rebellious age, and the devil is a musician, one who will give you songs that try to unravel what God gives you here. Not only that, but it will unravel your heart and life as well. Flee from him.

CHAPTER 8

Ordinary People With Voices

We have already noted the importance of recognizing the importance of what kind of occasion worship is, and therefore what kind of music should be presented to God. We have also noted the need for expertise. We come now to the question of what kind of people are to perform the music.

And the biblical answer is ordinary people. Because of who God is, and because we are offering our music to Him, it is necessary to offer Him the best *we* can do. And we should always be striving to grow and mature in our ability to present to Him the best we can do. But here, as in so many other places, there is a snare we must avoid.

Our covenant renewal form of worship is structured in terms of a meeting between God and His people. In some parts of the service, God is speaking through His ordained representatives, and the congregation listens. We have this in the sermon, in the Scripture reading, in the assurance of pardon, and in the benediction. Although mere mortals speak these words, they are doing so at God's behest and with His authority, which is why the congregation at such points simply hears, listens.

But the overwhelming characteristic of our response to Him is with music. We should present the best to Him, but what we are after is the entire congregation presenting their best.

If we select out the most musically gifted among us, and have them do the singing, the end result will be a liturgical dislocation—designated ministers singing at the people, instead of all the people singing to God. In Scripture, the sacrifice of praise is what we offer to Him.

This is why, for example, it may be a good idea to have the choir singing from the back. This is why we resist the idea of special performances from up front. This is why we want as many of you into the choir as we can get, and why we want as big a choir as we can get singing throughout the congregation throughout the entire service.

Given the nature of the case, the music should be offered to God by us, and we should strive to do well at it. But we should strive to do well at it as ones who have ordinary professions and lives, as ones who cannot perform musically at the level that some trained professionals can do.

CHAPTER 9

Three Kinds of Music

M usic can be divided into three general categories: music you should repent of, music you can grow from, and music you can grow into.

Music can be repented of for two reasons. The more obvious would be the intellectual musical attempts to declare the world to be a different kind of place than God created it to be. The music of Schoenberg and John Cage should be placed in this category.

Another form of repentance would be for thinking that any piece of music, provided *you* like it, should be suitable for any occasion. But the Bible teaches in multiple ways, that music is designed to *accompany*, and therefore there is one kind of music for mourning and another kind for dancing. There is music for worship, and there is music to get your guests chattering.

Music you can grow from is probably the kind of music you naturally gravitate to. Musically, it is not in rebellion against God—no non-Euclidean scales, everything is tonal, the rhythms are . . . rhythmical, and so forth. But in these days of mass production, most of it is pretty forgettable, and can almost be thought of as a consumption item. It is not sin, any more than Kraft Mac n' Cheese in a box is sin. But if you are still having that for every dinner fifteen years from now, it would be hard to escape the conclusion that you married the wrong person.

With the musical equivalent, the lyrics are trite and the melodic hooks are, if possible, even more trite. This is true of most popular music, but not all of it of course. Young people, if you like what you like, find the good stuff there, study it, think it through. Above everything else, do not define the "good stuff" as that which is currently hot.

What we want the music of the church to do is provide two things—a sense of the need for diverse music for diverse occasions, and an example of the kind of music that we should long to grow up into. What will music be like when it matures? What will music be like in the resurrection?

CHAPTER 10
Musical Education and the Future

As we seek to grow and mature in our understanding of music, and we learn more about the kind of music that best glorifies God in worship, we have to be careful to balance certain things.

The first thing is that we have to recognize where we are—we are living in a time when *general* musical education has been abandoned for some generations, with the result that many of us know what we like, but we don't know much what we are liking. So as we have undertaken the challenging task of musical reformation, we are trying to provide something to the next generation that we ourselves did not receive. Call this the old-dog-new-tricks problem. In the formation of a child's mind, many aspects of education are like pouring concrete—after a certain point, you are pretty much done.

But this is not a counsel of despair. In the first place, old dogs can learn more tricks than they might think. Rather than give up, sliding back into apathy, we need to accept the call to make a joyful noise the best we know how, and we don't have to recover all the lost years. We just have to learn a little bit more—that's all. God's grace establishes a principle that is as true here as it is everywhere else. God takes us from where we are, and not from where we should have been.

There is another aspect to this as well, another ground for encouragement. The way God has created the human race, another generation is always arriving. Fresh concrete trucks are always rolling up, and the concrete of *their* education is not hardened as ours is. The next generation need not be limited the same way we were.

Think of parents who were never educated, and who were unable to read. They know their limitations, and they can accept those limitations without accepting the same limitations for their children. Wise parents in this situation will sacrifice a great deal to provide the education that they know they were never provided. And it is the same kind of thing with music. If we are wise, the *real* musical reformation will grow up all around us.

CHAPTER 11
Music for Everyman

As we continue to learn the nature of body life, we have to understand the distinctions that are made between those with special gifts and all the rest of us who need to learn a basic competence in those gifts.

Not every Christian should be a scholar, but every Christian should know how to read. Not every Christian should be a vocational musician, but every Christian should know how to sing praises to God in public worship. Not every Christian should be able to parse the errors of second century Gnosticism, but every Christian should have learned contempt for gnosticism on an athletic field. Not every Christian should be a high level mathematician, but every Christian should know how to manage his own finances, balancing his own checkbook.

When Paul teaches us about body life, he is teaching us how the mature body functions, when those with developed gifts are exercising those gifts. But what do we do about the process of education, whereby we are training our children, discovering their areas of giftedness, and encouraging them in those areas? With developed gifts, we give way to one another. The eye sees on behalf of the ear, and the ear hears on behalf of the eye.

But when we are training our children, bringing them up to a basic competence in all these areas, we need to take care that we make room for them all. We make room for them all by refusing to make them competitors. This will keep the kids busy, but worse things than *that* have happened. Training in literacy is not at odds with musical training, training in sports is not at odds with academics, and so on, down the line.

CHAPTER 12

Initial Excitement and First Love

As we continue our journey into musical maturity, we have to remember something about *all* such journeys. The beginning of any worthwhile endeavor is always exciting. Whether it is the first day of school compared to a gray, school day three months later, or falling in love compared to faithfulness in a troubled patch of a marriage ten years later, the excitement of joining the army or navy compared to the smoke of battle, in all such endeavors we find high excitement at the beginning and the need for discipline later on.

In religious endeavors, we often mistake this early zeal for the Holy Spirit. Now of course the Spirit is sovereign, and He uses this zeal just as He can use anything else. But initial excitement is something that nonbelievers can have as well as us. In fact, Jesus even considered a particular kind of early zeal without the follow-through as something that was *characteristic* of non-belief (Mark 4:5).

When as a congregation we first set ourselves to the task of learning how to sing psalms, and how to sing in parts, that kind of excitement was certainly there. The Spirit was also there using it. But the danger lies in thinking that if that initial excitement cannot be sustained (which it cannot be), then *no* kind of long-term dedication is possible, which is false. There is a kind of love we are to have for God, and for one another, which is fervent constantly (1 Pet. 1:22). This doesn't run out.

Some of you recall the excitement of singing a new song, on a number of levels. But some others of you have grown up with this, and have never really known anything else. It is sometimes tempting to think you have to go off and do something else in order to have that initial excitement. But that is not how it works—the new song we have been given should be new and fresh for you as well.

CHAPTER 13
Finding Our Pitch

One of the things that pastors in the CREC have discussed, as we have worked through the problems that are confronting our congregations, is the challenge of psalm-singing fatigue. As we have set ourselves the challenge of learning to love the psalmody of the historic church, we have discovered that it is, like many valuable things, hard work.

For some it is hard because it is too much too fast. This stuff is way over their heads. For others it is hard because they are having to go so slow. They are eager for more, and frustrated by the pace. Others object to psalm selections, while others are just conservative and don't like changing things, period. In spite of all this, we have been greatly blessed as a congregation—we are blessed in the songs we are now able to sing, and we are almost equally as blessed by the songs we *used* to sing.

At the same time, we don't just want to hunker down and press on through—although there is a time and place for that strategy. We want to mix it up a bit, and experiment with ways of pushing ourselves in enjoyable ways, glorious, and God-honoring.

Remember that singing in harmony is only an adornment for those who live in harmony. As we do well, let us labor by God's grace to do even better, not growing weary in the good works He has given us to do. Those good works will include finding a parking spot, finding a seat, finding your neighbor, and finding your pitch.

CHAPTER 14

Monks in the Cloister

A brief word should be said in defense of the occasional chant. The point of learning to chant is not so that we can all start sounding spooky and ethereal, like monks in the cloister. The point is more straightforward than that. The apostle Paul tells us that we are to let the Word of Christ dwell in us *richly*. We want to internalize as much of the Word of God as we can, and chant is a wonderful (and relatively simple) way to do this.

In our congregation, we have been singing psalms for many years. We have done some chanting, but most of what we have learned is made up of metrical psalms. This is all to the good, and it is part of the glory of Trinitarian worship. Hymns and metrical psalms are here to stay. But we want this to be balanced. With a metrical psalm, the text submits to the authority of the tune. The tune stays put, and the text gives way. With a chant, it is the other way. The tune submits to the authority of the text.

Because there are fewer than ten basic chant tones, when you come to learn a new text, you can just take one of those chant tones, and apply it to that new text. And as you learn it rightly, practicing at home, you will not sound like a monk in the cloister, but more like a Presbyterian in the shower.

CHAPTER 15

Every Lawful Door

We should be eager to establish and grow up into a genuine musical literacy as a congregation, as a community. But we have to take care to understand this process rightly. We obviously have to teach our children, and we have a great deal to learn ourselves in this process. And in this area, we have set our hand to the plow. But we must take care—there are certain things that are *not* meant by musical literacy promoted by the church.

We can understand this by analogy—the Protestant emphasis in the history of the West has been a great boon. Because we are people of the *Word*, it has been the most natural thing in the world for us to be people of *words*. Because we want our children to have access to the Word of God, we make a special point of teaching them all how to read. But of course, once we have opened up the Scriptures for them, they go on to read (and write) many other things. The Scriptures are the center, not the periphery. Because we know the centrality of the Word, we can enjoy many other kinds of literature—from haiku to *The Lord of the Rings*—throughout the rest of our lives. But when the centrality of Scripture is lost, then uninspired letters cannot avoid disintegration. This is why public letters in our nation are the in middle of a five-spiral crash.

It is the same principle with the music of the church. Man was created to worship God, and to praise him with song. Because this is what we were made for, we want to teach our children how to do it. This is the central motive. We want them to be able to do much more as worshiping Christians than we have been able to do. The songs we sing here *are the most important music in our lives*, and should be treated that way. This is the center of our music. But when we have been equipped to do what God calls us to do here, we discover that the musical abilities we have acquired remain with us through the rest of the week. We don't just retain the songs—we retain the literacy.

Do a thought experiment. Imagine a generation from now a community that has virtually a one hundred percent musical literacy rate. Suppose that all the children under the age of ten today are able then to read a new hymn or psalm at sight. Do you honestly think that this will produce a monotonous sameness in all the music that is sung by those people throughout the week? On the contrary, we are perilously close to a monotonous sameness *now*. But when church music recovers its rightful place, it will do for all kinds of music what literacy does for every book in the library. It will open every lawful door.

CHAPTER 16

Shared Principles

As we seek to cultivate our understanding of the kind of music we should be offering to God—and the corollary of what we as a congregation should be learning how to perform—we bump into another challenge.

Church musicians come up against a greater challenge than other artists do. Some of this is a help and some of it is a great hindrance, and we need to work through it. Poets, and sculptors, and painters, and such generally do not face much amateur competition. But in the realm of music, virtually everyone is either a performer or a DJ with a listening audience of one. We are (all of us) surrounded by music all the time; we create our own playlists, we form our own bands, we write our own songs, and we form our own decided opinions. Nothing wrong with any of this, but the fact that virtually everyone handles music and decides on music does create a set of challenges.

Now we want the music we learn how to offer to God to become the driving music that informs the rest of our music. This does not mean that our folk music, or our high end music, will be stylistically identical to what we do here. But all creational music shares the same principles—it will be tonal, it will be rhythmic, it will be melodic, and so forth. Blues, jazz and folk build on the same creational foundation, even though stylistically they are not appropriate for what we do here.

So when we try to sort out what kind of music we use in worship, we distinguish between two different kinds of "inappropriate." One is inappropriate because of the kind of occasion this is, not because there is anything wrong with the music itself. You wouldn't play romantic mood music at a kindergartner's birthday party, and you wouldn't play a lively ragtime piece here. But there is another kind of music, sadly popular even among Christians, that is inappropriate here because it is inappropriate everywhere. Music that is cacophonous all the way down, or dissonant all the way through, is not to be relegated to a certain part of your life—rather it is to be repented of.

CHAPTER 17
Importing Music to the Church

When we worship, we are a gathered assembly, gathered in order to worship the Lord. But we have gathered out of a community, a group of people who live together, serving the Lord in various capacities, throughout the rest of the week. What we do *there* is what we bring *here*. We see this in everything.

The Lord blesses us financially on Wednesday, and so we bring our tithes and offerings here on the Lord's day. Our children are receiving a biblical education, and so when I am preaching I can assume a certain amount of biblical literacy. We are building the Temple here, but the sound of the chisel is not heard here.

The same principle applies to music and music education. As Christians we value words highly because we are people of the Word. We teach our children to read because we want Bible reading to be at the center of their lives. But a large portion of our worship service is musical. We sing a lot. Coming to this offering prepared is far better than coming to it unprepared. And preparing for musical worship involves far more than a simple heads up on what songs will be sung, although that is a small part of it. Musical education is like the rest of education; it is cumulative, and it takes years.

This means that parents should be as interested in musical education for their children as they are in basic literacy. This may be chorus at school, individual training in singing, or private piano lessons, or violin lessons, or any number of other options. Far more is involved than individual self-improvement. Over the course of the next generation, this will be a major contribution to the reformation of worship in the Church.

CHAPTER 18

Incarnational Music

We know what the Incarnation is—the eternal Word became flesh and dwelt among us. But what does it mean for us to be or become incarnational? What is it of ours that can take on flesh the way the Lord did, even if it is a dim imitation?

There are two things to note at first. The first is that the Lord became a man in a great act of humility, and the second is that that which could not be seen or handled became tangible or concrete. A great artist who carves a magnificent statue in arrogance and pride is not being incarnational. A retiring individual who, in the name of humility, never does anything concrete or specific, is not being incarnational.

Now when we sing, as with all the arts, we are making something tangible. Something that did not exist before is now taking shape. If we do it with grace and humility, then the song we sing is incarnational. If we sing with the tongues of angels, but have no love, the result is just a mingle-mangle. If we have love, but never express it, we actually have no love.

Now when the Lord stooped to become a man, the greatness of the miracle involved was in an inverse relationship to the distance He covered. The greatness of the miracle—for which He will be forever praised—was made possible by how much He had to stoop.

In the same way, when we sing the glories of God in simple tunes, with three chords, this is not an insult to Him. This is part of the point. Provided the great thing is done, the glory of God is displayed.

Musical archangels who refuse to stoop do not display God's glory. But roly poly bugs who think that it all begins and ends with them are just refusing to stoop from a much lower place. God's wisdom is seen in this—He brings high and low together, unity and diversity together, simple and complex together. And it is in Christ that all things hold together.

CHAPTER 19

Striving for Permanence

A s Christians, we hold to the doctrine of *creatio ex nihilo*, creation from nothing. God spoke and it was. But we are not Deists; we do not believe that God created a static thing, capable of ongoing existence by itself. God did not create the heavens and the earth, and then walk away. In His providential care, He sustains it. In Christ, Paul says, all things hold together, all things consist (Col. 1:17). In Hebrews 1:3, we are told that God continues to uphold all things by the word of His power. This is *creatio continua*.

But this doctrine of an ongoing sustaining of the created order includes another aspect. God created man to be the steward of His creation, and He gave us great responsibilities in this regard. Our rebellion and sin in Eden crippled us in our abilities to fulfill the creation mandate, but in Christ God has restored everything in principle. The Great Commission is a reiteration of our responsibility, as first announced to Adam, and repeated again to Noah. This means, as Paul says, that our labor in the Lord is *not* in vain (1 Cor. 15:58). What we do here matters. The work we do matters. This is not limited to ethical good works; it includes *cultural* good works.

In music, what we sing matters. The way we sing it matters. What we compose matters. In the resurrection, we will be given a new song, but this does not mean that the old songs will be taken away. Too often, evangelical Christians throw up their cultural achievements like makeshift scaffolding. We think, "It's all gonna burn, man," and so what we do here does not matter. But as Paul teaches us in 1 Corinthians 3, *some* of it is going to burn, but other aspects of what we do in ministry will be tested and purified. Some of our hymns will be with us in the resurrection. Rather than trying to guess which ones, we need to turn our attention to all of them, with an educated desire for all of them to glorify the Lamb as worthy, "the Lamb that was slain."

We should sing as though we wanted all of them to make the cut.

CHAPTER 20

Tabernacle of David

We have seen that Paul assumes the use of musical instruments in worship—we are to sing psalms, hymns and spiritual songs with all our hearts, and we are to make melody as we do by means of instruments. Because this has been controversial in the church over the centuries, perhaps we should say a few more things about the use of instruments.

Instrumental music was not part of the requirements of the law for the tabernacle and later the Temple. As first established, the sacrificial system was silent. The first great innovation came with David, who established the tabernacle of David (2 Sam. 6:17), in which the primary sacrifice was musical, instruments included. Later, when Solomon built the Temple, the music of the tabernacle located on Mt. Zion was transferred to the Temple, along with the name of Zion—even though the Temple was not actually on Zion. We have no record of instrumental music in synagogues, while the instrumental music in the Temple came there from the tabernacle of David. This tabernacle was a type of the Christian church, as James noted at the Jerusalem Council. "After this I will return, and will build again the tabernacle of David, which is fallen down; and I will build again the ruins thereof, and I will set it up" (Acts 15:16). The chief characteristic of this tabernacle was that of musical praise, accompanied by instruments.

So the musical instrumentation of the Old Testament was not a fading shadow of the older order, but rather a glorious anticipation of the new order—which we are privileged to be part of. This brings us back to Paul's exhortation—as we have been given this privilege, we need to take great care that we don't come to it in a perfunctory way. We must sing and make melody with all our hearts, with all our might—with the same attitude David had as he worshiped at the consecration of this tabernacle.

CHAPTER 21

Joyful Noise

We should be familiar with the exhortation that music in worship is summoned to be *skillful* music (Ps. 33:3). We are not permitted to just throw anything together and call it good. But skill is not the only characteristic we are told to cultivate. "Sing unto him a new song; play skillfully *with a loud noise*" (Ps. 33:3).

There is a temptation when churches pursue excellence in music, and that is the very real temptation to become music snobs. And when *that* happens, a party spirit sets in and we start feeling superior to those who praise God with three chords maximum. But holding on to what we know about musical excellence, what do these brothers and sisters do that is better than how we do it? Well, frequently, contemporary worship music is *louder* than what we do. This is a clear and identifiable superiority.

The Bible says that we are to worship God with shouts, with cymbals, with percussion, with *noise*. This is as much a biblical standard as that of playing skillfully—all the earth is to make a loud noise and rejoice (Ps. 98: 4); the cymbals are to be loud (Ps. 150:5); those who trust in God are to shout for joy (Ps. 5: 11); God ascends with a shout (Ps. 47:5).

God does not just want quality in music; He wants quantity. He wants *volume*. And to take pride in the quality if it is mumbled is just as wrong headed as to take pride in the noise apart from excellence in execution. We don't get to pick and choose, and we don't get to lord it over those who pick and choose to privilege a different deficiency. Adulterers on Mondays and Wednesdays do not get to feel superior to adulterers who sin on Tuesdays and Fridays.

So clap your hands, all you peoples, shout unto God with a voice of triumph.

CHAPTER 22

Music for the World

The songs of the saints are not a rehearsal in an empty theater. And although the Scripture says that we *do* address one *another* in psalms and hymns and spiritual songs, we have to remember that the music of God's people is not private music. We address God, and we address one another, but others overhear. This is public music, music for the world.

Jesus said that the Church was a city on a hill, one that could not be hidden away. He instructed us not to take the Church, a light for the world, and hide it under a bushel. We have unfortunately taken this saying and restricted it to the level of individual application—not that that application is wrong in itself, mind you. You as an individual ought not to hide your light under a bushel. But the light Jesus was speaking of here was made up of His disciples collectively. He was speaking of His city, His nation, His people, and His Church. And collectively we are not just to be visible—we are also to be *audible*. A bushel is objectionable because it not only makes light invisible, it also muffles sound.

Our task is to sing to God and to one another, with a periodic and regular invitation given to the nations to listen, and to join in. The music of the saints is evangelistic in that sense. Now to be evangelistic, we do not have to go and sing to them directly, although we sometimes do—as when we go out to sing Christmas carols in places like the mall. Our music is evangelistic every Lord's day, when we sing psalms in such a way that the Lord is able to use them to glorify His name in a particular region.

Your neighbors know that you are here now, singing. The Lord of all music is able to take that simple fact, and unsettle those who have no real music as the center of their lives. Sing as though an invitation were contained in it, because there is one. Sing, and let the Lord be the sound engineer. Let Him determine what gets heard and by whom. Our task is to sing with that understanding.

CHAPTER 23
A New Song

In multiple places in Scripture, we are told of the blessing that comes with singing a new song. But this is an easy phrase to misunderstand—we tend to think it means a *recent* song. But the idea of the new song is that of a fresh song. It refers the quality of the song, and the quality of the singing. A song composed ten minutes ago could be sung as though it were a dirge, and a song grounded in the ancient wisdom before the foundation of the world—worthy is the Lamb that was slain—is new every morning.

But of course, if we in our lethargy and sloth sing the ancient glories like we were dragging a wet rope, then we are slandering the good news by our musical behavior. And the quality we are looking for does not come primarily from the diaphragm, throat, and mouth, but rather from the *heart*. If we have an attitude about the music, then whatever it is we sing, whenever it was composed, it is not the new song that Scripture talks about.

Now I need to directly state one implication of this. This means that to the extent we avoid what is called contemporary music for our worship services, this is not because it is contemporary at all. It is because as a general rule we believe most music in that category does not offer the same scope that other music offers for singing the new song that God sets before us. It is too limited. In saying this, we are not saying that a song that does offer the scope will be one that the congregation will necessarily take advantage of. We frequently do not, and so the point is to stir you up to love and good notes.

Many contemporary services are full of saints whose hearts surpass their music. If we are not careful, we will stumble so that our hearts lag far behind our music. If that happens, and it has happened many times in the history of the church, we should take solemn warning. It would be far, far better to be someone who did not have the musical vocabulary for his heart than to be someone who did not have the heart for his musical vocabulary.

One other thing. You probably picked up that there was an implied musical criticism of much contemporary Christian music in what I just said. Because contemporary Christian music gets a bad rap from all directions, I would like to add an exhortation. Too many young people turn up their noses at contemporary Christian music (because they hear such criticisms), but then they turn to secular music that has all of the faults of contemporary Christian music, and none of the virtues. And once they have settled there, they are deaf to all criticisms, which shows what is actually happening.

CHAPTER 24

Musical Giftedness

O n the physical level, the whole body is involved in singing, and in making music with various instruments. This means there is something else to remember as we pursue musical reformation in our congregation.

The apostle Paul addresses a common problem with body life, a mistake that is easy to make. That is the mistake of thinking that the function of a set of gifts, one member or organ in the body, is determinative of what the rest of the body should be doing. But each set of gifts is *on behalf of* the rest of the body, and not to be understood as the *destiny* of the rest of the body. The eyes see for the rest of the body, which does not mean the rest of the body is destined to become an eyeball. If the whole body were an eye, where would the hearing be?

We really want to mature in our ability to make music before the Lord. But we don't want to do it at the expense of all the other things that God has equipped bodies to do. We don't want to pursue excellence here in such a way as to produce an ecclesiastical version of an *idiot savant*, extraordinarily gifted in one way, and worthless in most others.

The work of the body involves hands, ears, eyes, mouth, and so on. Each part happily contributes its function, and indeed *insists* on contributing what God has given. But each part must also be cautioned against becoming imperialistic—demanding that the whole body place the same value on that particular gift that the gifted parts do.

Now of course, Paul was addressing the matter of spiritual gifts when he taught us this principle—exhortation, encouragement, teaching, helps, and so on. But how much more should we see it as applicable when it comes to other common gifts that God has given to men generally. The principle applies to music, to architecture, to literary taste, to business expertise, to educational expertise, and so on. We all need each other.

As a congregation, we want to grow and mature across the range of our humanity, and not to grow in any lopsided way. This means that we will grow more slowly in our musical maturation than we might like—and there will be a certain element of driving the musicians among us crazy in the meantime—but this is best in the long run. We are growing oak trees, not cabbages.

CHAPTER 25

Music and Lyrics Together

In the modern world, we have come to think of music as one thing and "the words" as quite another thing. They may complement one another, like ham and eggs, but they are also separable and distinct. We therefore have instrumental music only, and we have poetry, or lofty speech. If the poetry is high, or devotional, and if it scans, it might be set to music.

Because we have drifted into this mindset we have come to think that church music should be evaluated in two separate ways. We evaluate the music according to the canons of music, and we evaluate the lyrics (if we do) in accordance with the canons of poetry—resulting in the kind of observation that C. S. Lewis once offered, which was that church music was ninth-rate poetry set to third-rate music.

But in the Bible, the words and music were much more organically intertwined—we are told to sing psalms, and hymns and spiritual songs. The words or lyrics are not an optional add-on, but are an integral part of the song. Words are not this pedestrian thing that we sometimes decorate with music, as we occasional decorate a dining room for a birthday party. Rather, words are not understood *as words* unless they are frequently sung.

As we are growing in our understanding of congregational music, this means that we are not just amateur musicians, we are also amateur poets, and poetry reciters. I am using the word *amateur* here, not in its modern sense of incompetent part-timer, but rather in the original sense of one who pursues his love for the sake of that love, and not because he is being paid.

We must reflect on the music, and we must reflect on the words, and since we cannot concentrate on more than one thing at a time, we can do that separately. But we must always remember that in worship the two form an artistic whole. The words are not just filler, acceptable just so long as they don't say anything positively wrong. They are as much a part of the artistry as the music, and they are part of what we are called to grow and mature in.

CHAPTER 26
When the Fire Falls

One of the things we should notice in Scripture is the close association of the music of the people of God and the nations of men. There is a regular appeal, throughout Scripture, asking the nations to hear us when we sing.

The music of the saints, rightly done, is universal and evangelistic. The music of the saints, wrongly done, becomes "church music," set off in a ghetto of its own—perhaps to be respected and perhaps despised, but always isolated. Many a country singer claims to have roots in "gospel," over there, but the point is more isolation than simple distinction. There are musical similarities, to be sure, but we are careful to maintain genre walls.

If our music is not having an effect upon the nations, we cannot change it by tinkering with the notes, or finding better songs. Rather, we need to sing to God, with overflowing hearts, and with a true and living faith in the gospel of Jesus Christ, and if we do, the music will do what only the Spirit of God can do with it. If we do not have faith in the gospel (by which I of course mean vibrant faith), then the better the music gets, the more we will sound like trained professionals.

There is a difference between efficiency and blessing. One man with five talents blessed is going to be more potent than a man with one talent unblessed, or ten talents unblessed, for that matter. Our business, in the first instance, therefore, is to seek for the blessing. Talent is not enough. Training is not enough. Learning the songs is not enough. As we have undertaken the task of musical reformation in our church, all we have been doing is assembling materials on the altar, in the earnest expectation that God will cause the fire to come down. Some of the more difficult songs we have learned are the sea water that Elijah poured out on the altar.

Without the fire, it doesn't matter. And when the fire falls, in a completely different kind of way, it doesn't matter either.

CHAPTER 27

The Riptide Issue

So I take it as a given that God can be worshiped and genuinely glorified, in a Lord's Day service, with different styles of music, and with different kinds of instrumentation. I do not say any style of music, but I do say different styles of music. Some music is of course excluded because it is lawless, and other kinds of music should be excluded because it is an appropriate kind of music for a different sort of occasion entirely. The music is fine, but not now, not here. I have argued elsewhere for what we are seeking to do musically at Christ Church on that basis.

But there is an additional consideration as well, what I call the "riptide" issue. I do not mean to limit the possible discussion to the two forms of music I will discuss, but am just using them for purposes of illustration.

These are the two kinds of music we can use in our thought experiment—traditional and ecclesiastical on the one hand, and contemporary on the other. I have seen and heard God genuinely glorified with both kinds of music, but (having been around) I have also seen both kinds gone bad. And therein lies the riptide problem.

Let us define traditional and ecclesiastical as including hymns, organs, stateliness, accomplished choir pieces, and so on. Let us define contemporary as including guitars, drum sets, worship bands, and so on. I trust we all have the general picture. Both of these can be done right, and both can be done wrong. When traditional music goes wrong, it can manifest itself in things like a prissy fastidiousness, effeminacy, perfectionism, elitism in the choir, and a organist with an acoustical rock pile to bury the congregation with. When contemporary music goes wrong, it can manifest itself in acute hipsterism, worship leaders whose facial expressions are more suggestive of masturbation than devotion, elitism in the worship band, and a lead guitarist with an acoustical rock pile to bury the congregation with.

Ironically, both wrong forms tend to squeeze out the full participation of the congregation in order to turn the event into a rock concert and/or organ recital. Traditionalism gone wrong lands you with an organist who brings his silk pink slippers in order to play with the footsie pedals. Contemporism gone wrong lands you with a worship leader who pats his chest in orgasmic ecstasy as the Em/C chord change approaches.

Now, here is the difficulty. When a church opts for one approach or the other, they obviously have to deal with the potential errors that accompany their choice, the one they have made. And along the beach of church music today, you do have to go swimming *somewhere*. In my judgment, at the stretch of beach called contemporary there is a massive riptide that has drowned a thousand aspiring musicians for every one we have lost at St. Olaf's Reef. The temptations of previous generations are not the ones we have to grapple with.

CHAPTER 28
A Final Caution

Our musical goal should be to do the most we can do to glorify God in our music. That being the case, we ought not to accept any artificial ceiling that will limit what we will be able to do. It is my conviction that, while contemporary or folk forms of music are certainly *lawful* to present to God in worship, they do have the effect of creating such a ceiling. They have a tendency to restrict our options, along with our ability to grow, in a way that more developed church music does not need to do.

Now musicians, God bless them, are opinionated (unlike the present writer). This means that everyone will have to work with me here in a thought experiment that requires accomplished musicians who are extraordinarily docile, and who will play just what we tell them so we can hear what it sounds like. It is only a thought experiment, so they shouldn't mind too much.

Traditional church music is far more *inclusive* than contemporary is. Put simply, a church that has a choir that can perform Bach cantatas has a choir that can also sing gospel, or spirituals, folk hymns, and so forth. A church that has a worship band does not have the ability to upgrade to a cantata. Their options are far more limited. At the same time, the musicians who can go broad like this are frequently very reluctant to do so. Highly trained church musicians are certainly *capable* of including different kinds of music, but often do not because they are *bigoted* against that kind of music at all. They see it as the camel's nose under the edge of the tent. But this reservation is mental or emotional, not musical.

Contemporary church music, on the other hand, is led by broad minded people who do not have the musical vocabulary to act out their broad-mindedness. Their *minds* are broad enough, but their musical range is *narrow*. They would be happy to do the cantata if they could . . . but they can't. The bass player isn't up to it.

The metaphor of a big tent has been used a great deal, but it is too often missed that a big tent requires a big pole to hold the whole thing up. It is my conviction that in the musical reformation of the church the only thing that will serve for this pole is classic, historic, traditional church music, of the kind that requires church musicians trained at the graduate level. If that is there, we can (and should) make the tent as big as we please, including all kinds of music that the Spirit has given to the church over the years. In doing this, we have to guard against training church musicians who think that life in the tent means standing right next to the pole. We should want their minds to be as broad as their musical ability is. They are the ones who have the musical authority to incorporate all sorts of musical genres.

But if we lose that pole, we lose the whole tent. At the end of that process, we will find ourselves singing a dark little blanket fort, assembled out of the three blankets of G, C, and D^7.

www.ingramcontent.com/pod-product-compliance
Lightning Source LLC
Chambersburg PA
CBHW060535030426
42337CB00021B/4275